Length: approx. 646 km
Recommended time

BORDE

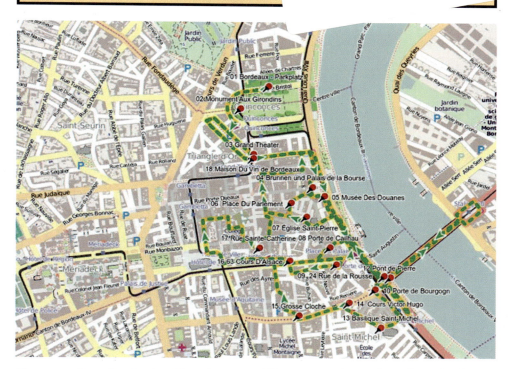

Our route starts in Bordeaux. If you arrive the day before, there are two campgrounds in the vicinity of Bordeaux:

Camping Beausoleil GPS: N44 45.360 W0 37.620
Camping Bel Air GPS: N44 46.999 W0 22.220

From both campsites, depending on the time of the day, you are in the city center in about half an hour.

Waypoint(WP) 01: Bordeaux-Parking

GPS: N44 50.784 W0 34.404

The easiest way to find a parking lot is at this POI. The car is parked in the shade, parking fee has to be paid and from here you can easily start a tour of the city by walking.

The tour takes about three hours, without visiting museums. The following two maps show the route.

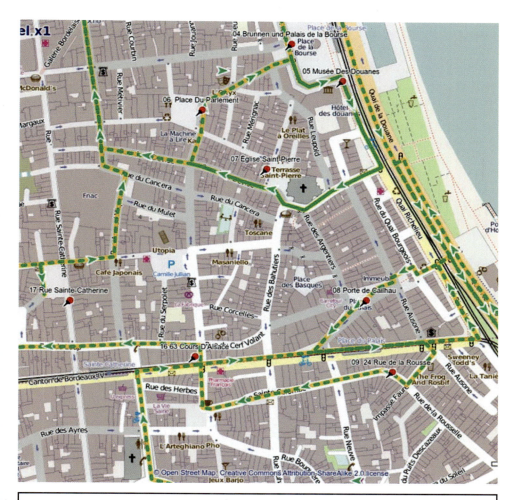

WP 02: Monument Aux Girondins

GPS: N44 50.720 W0 34.517

Right at the parking the first sight is located. Overall, the Monument aux Gerodins reaches with more than 50 meters into the sky. The monument commemorates the executed Girondins in 1792, who fought against centralism and demanded more independence for their town. That's why many of them were arrested and executed. They are named Girondists because most of them came from the Department Gironde around Bordeaux. The monument is a recent one, it was not built until the late 19th Century. The really great artistic monument has wells on either side of the column. On the north side of the fountain the statue symbolizes harmony between farmers, citizens and workers, the fountain dedicated to the southern side, symbolizes the triumph of the Republic. 4 horses pull a triumphal cart out of the water. The allegories Falsehood, ignorance and Lie, however drown in the floods. The symbolism is very dominant, the statues are really finest art.

WP 03: Grand Theater
GPS: N44 50.586 W0 34.463

It is considered one of the most beautiful cultural venues in France and was built by the Parisian architect Victor Louis. The 12 pillars provide the ancient atmosphere and contribute to the elegance of the building. In the extension of the pillars on the palustrade there are statues, that symbolize the muses. The theater was built between 1775-1780 by initiative of Cardinal Richelieu. Obvious is the affection of the architect for ancient Greece, which he displayed not only at the 88-meter-wide facade, but also inside the cultural center.

WP 04: Fountain and Palais la Bourse
GPS: N44 50.488 W0 34.226

Impressive is the Place de la Bourse with the Palais de la Bourse and the Customs Museum, in the center is the central fountain with the 3 Graces.

WP 05: Musée Des Douanes - Museum

GPS: N44 50.462 W0 34.177

WP 06: Place Du Parlement

GPS: N44 50.442 W0 34.311

Nice square in the heart of Bordeauxs.

WP 07: Église Saint-Pierre

GPS: N44 50.401 W0 34.249

In the district of St. Pierre there is a less historically significant, but very idyllic church, the Eglise St. Pierre. It nestles quietly in the small square which is an insider tip for good food and reasonably priced restaurants.

WP 08: Porte de Cailhau

GPS: N44 50.308 W0 34.154

Impressing are the medieval city gates, as the Porte Cailhau on the banks of the Garonne. It dates from the 15th Century and can be visited inside as well. It was completed in 1495. Charles VIII had just won the battle of Fornoue and the original gate was remodel as a triumphal arch. Originally, the gate was the entrance to Chateau de l Ombriere, which does not exist anymore. Unusually are the 4 tower hoods, with which the gate reaches a height of 34 meters.

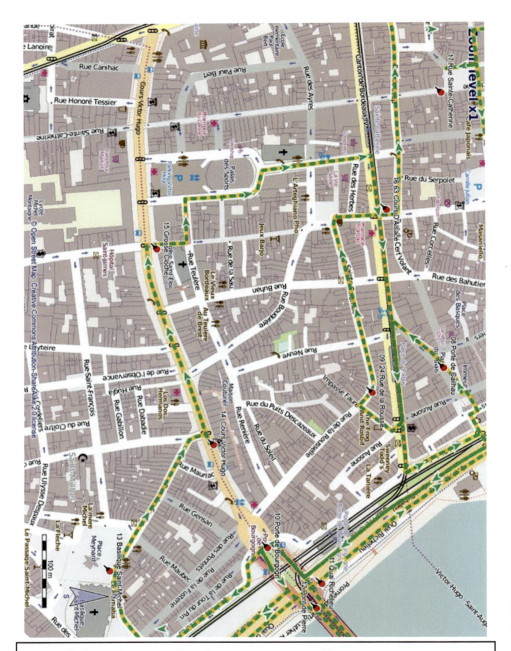

WP 09: Rue de la Rousselle

GPS: N44 50.258 W0 34.128

The Rue de la Rousselle was earlier a shopping street. Here, several traders had settled, especially wine and grain dealers.

WP 10: Porte de Bourgogne
GPS: N44 50.184 W0 33.971

On the extension of the Pont de Pierre to the Old Town to the Cours Victor Hugo there is the Porte des Salinieres from the mid 18th century, which was formerly called Porte de Bourgogne.

WP 11: Quai Richelieu
GPS: N44 50.222 W0 33.934

One of the busiest roads along the Garonne, the Qai Richelieu with the wonderful skyline.

WP 12: Pont de Pierre
GPS: N44 50.219 W0 33.909

It is the oldest bridge in Bordeaux. Napoleon I needed for his Spanish campaign an effective way of crossing the river. The ferrymen were not able to cope with the huge amounts of war material, so there had to be built a bridge. 1810 therefore a wooden construction was built, which was replaced in 1821 by a stone construction. From the bridge, you have a very good view of the skyline.

WP 13: Basilique Saint-Michel

GPS: N44 50.074 W0 33.948

Around the Basilica St. Michel there is always hustle and bustle. The 114 meter high bell tower, La Fleche, which means "arrow" points into the sky and can be walked up to a height of 47 meters. It was built from 1472 to 1492.

WP 14: Cours Victor Hugo

GPS: N44 50.147 W0 34.075

Only a few steps away from St. Michel is Cours Victor Hugo, a typical French street with old buildings and interesting shops. Strolling down the street just after 100m you are in front of the symbol of the city, the Porte de la Grosse Cloche.

WP 15: Grosse Cloche
GPS: N44 50.107 W0 34.277

Originally the building was the town hall tower, which later served as the city gate. The name comes from the big 8 ton bell in the middle. The clock was installed in 1759, the bell in 1775. The bell was rung before for special occasions, such as the beginning of the grape harvest. The tower dates from the 15th Century and was built on the remains of an older gate. The central part is flanked by two 41-meter towers.

WP 16: Cours D'Alsace
GPS: N44 50.269 W0 34.316

Busy shopping street.

WP 17: Cathedral Saint Andre
GPS: N44 50.307 W0 34.436

A little apart from the church is the bell tower of the Cathedral of Saint Andre, the reason, because they feared that by the vibrations of the bell, the cathedral could be destroyed. On the top there is now a gilded statue of Notre Dame d'Aquitaine, which since 1863 adorns the top. Originally, the tower had a 12 meter high peak, which was destroyed by a storm in 1667. The tower is named after Archbishop Pey - Berland, who initiated it. Between 1440 and 1446 it was built in the Gothic style. Not less beautiful is the Cathedrale Staint-Andre itself, though not entirely without problems. First there were serious problems with the financing, the vaults were later threatened with collapse, hence the extra bell. Later, a fire destroyed the cathedral. 30 years later, repeated destruction during the revolution.

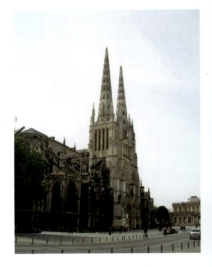

WP 18: Maison Du Vin de Bordeaux

GPS: N44 50.573 W0 34.462

Also interesting is the tapered shape of the Maison du Vin, which is dedicated to the famous Bordeaux wine that can be tasted here.

Bordeaux - Chât.Pichon-Longueville - Chât. Cos D'Estournel - Moulin de Vensac - Le gurp - Hourtin Plage - Lanacau Ocean   204 km

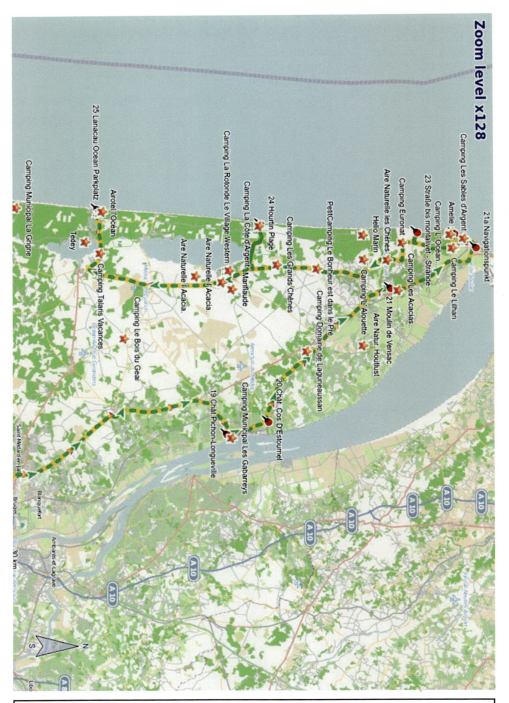

Camping Municipal Les Gabarreys
GPS: N45 11.109 W0 44.531

WP 19: Chât.Pichon-Longueville

GPS: N45 10.606 W0 45.079

As soon as you leave the city, one wine chateaux after the other. Chateau Pichon offers simplicity. It can be visited daily, including wine tasting. The vineyards of the Chateau are 70 hectars and benefit from the warm humid and sunny climate. In Bordeaux are only produced wines, which are mixtures of different grapes called cuvées. Here 60% of the grapes are Cabernet Sauvignon, 36% Merlot, 4% Cabernet Franc and 1% Petit Verdot which are blended to cuvées.

WP 20: Chât. Cos D'Estournel

GPS: N45 13.979 W0 46.598

This is a truly strange Chateau. From the outside, one would think that this castle is somewhere in the Orient, with turrets and ornaments out of 1001 Nights.

Camping Domaine de Laguneaussan
GPS: N45 17.220 W0 54.840

Camping Les Acacias
GPS: N45 24.617 W1 02.122

WP 21: Moulin de Vensac

GPS: N45 23.851 W1 02.475

In Vensac you should visit the wonderful small windmill. It can be visited as part of guided tours on weekends. Demonstrated are the operation of the mill and the miller's tools. Interesting is the sailcloth, which is mounted on each wing and is rolled when the mill is not in operation. The mill of Vensac is one of the few that has survived fully functional.

WP 21a: Navigation Point
GPS: N45 30.775 W1 07.236

This navigation point, leads you via Soulac-sur-Mer to the coast. The place is nice, the bakery in the pedestrian zone provides absolutely delicious delicacies for you.

WP 22: Le Gurp - Strand
GPS: N45 29.091 W1 09.009

Beautiful beach with a parking lot, where you can spend the night, it is an official RV park.

WP 23: Beaches

GPS: N45 26.045 W1 09.157

Beaches here are countless, and this is beautiful as well, although without infrastructure, such as toilets or showers.

Amelie GPS: N45 28.950 W1 09.033

Camping L' Océan GPS: N45 28.819 W1 08.738

Camping Le Lilhan GPS: N45 29.134 W1 07.101

Camping Les Lacs GPS: N45 29.011 W1 07.136

Camping Euronat GPS: N45 24.976 W1 07.794

Aire Naturelle les Chênes
GPS: N45 23.756 W1 05.676

Camping L' Alouette GPS: N45 21.843 W1 05.824

Helio Marin GPS: N45 21.783 W1 08.750

Petit Camping Le Bonheur
GPS: N45 18.060 W1 04.740

Camping Les Grands Chênes
GPS: N45 14.820 W1 05.220

Camping La Côte d'Argent.
GPS: N45 13.378 W1 09.879

WP 24: Hourtin Plage /Hourtin

GPS: N45 13.379 W1 10.221

A typical village on the Atlantic coast is Hourtin. A small church, a large central square, bakers, butchers and La Poste, that's all - quiet life. The towns on the coast are often divided. There is the original place like here, for example Hourtin - Bourg, often the villages have the addition "Ville" in their names. Over the time on the coast, ports or tourist centers developed, which were then given supplements like "plague", or "Ocean" or "Port". In the case of Hourtin, there is Hourtin - Bourg, Hourtin Plage and Hourtin Port.

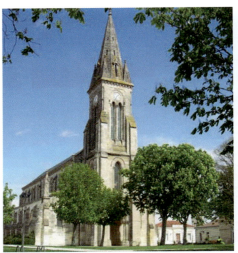 

| Camping Les Ourmes
GPS: N45 10.926 W1 04.538 |
|---|
| Camping La Rotonde Le Village Western
GPS: N45 10.767 W1 04.474 |
| Mariflaude GPS: N45 11.167 W1 02.367 |
| Camping L' Orée du Bois.
GPS: N45 10.340 W1 03.178 |
| Aire Naturelle l' Acacia
GPS: N45 08.220 W1 03.900 |

WP 25: Lanacau Ocean Parking

GPS: N45 00.134 W1 12.100

The surfer's paradise is Lacanau - Ocean, meeting place of the youth at the Atlantic Coast. Here they are surfing from dawn to dusk. On a plastic board, the young people jump into the waves to to ride back on top of a wave back to the shore, despite cool water, but the wetsuits keep the cold away. The town has adapted to the audience. Colorful houses line the main street, a pub follows another, creperie, pizzeria, cocktail bars and at night is party time.

Lanacau Ocean - Cap Ferret - Le Teich - Arcachon - Dune du Pilat - Biscarosse Plage 157 km

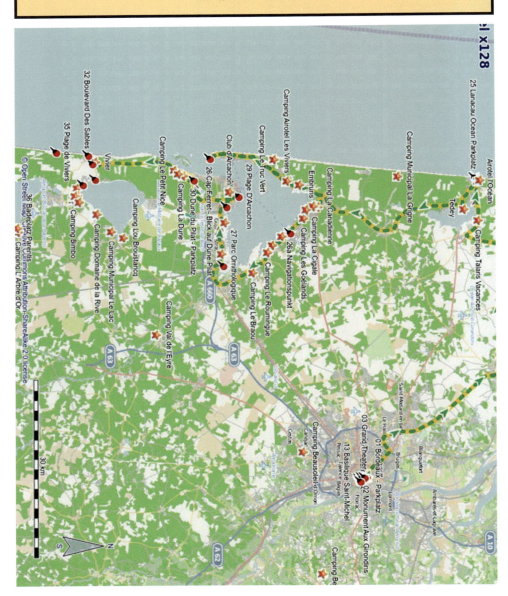

WP 26: Cap Ferret - View of Dune Pilat

GPS: N44 37.340 W1 14.835

From Cap Ferret one has a magnificent view of the Dune du Pilat. The peninsula looks sophisticated and is certainly one of the most visited areas on the Atlantic coast.

Campsites round the basin:

Camping Le Truc Vert
GPS: N44 42.930 W1 14.573

Camping Airotel Les Viviers
GPS: N44 44.063 W1 11.759

Embruns GPS: N44 45.100 W1 11.233

Camping La Canadienne
GPS: N44 46.717 W1 08.582

Camping La Cigale GPS: N44 46.374 W1 08.528

Camping Pasteur GPS: N44 45.714 W1 08.221

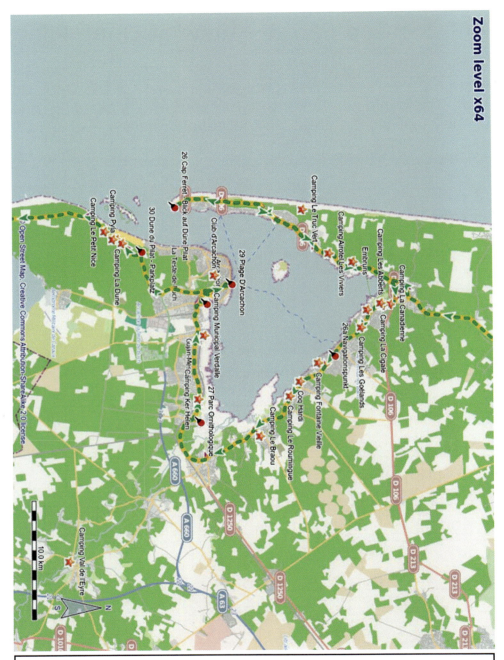

WP 26a: Navigation Point
GPS: N44 44.242 W1 05.367

Most navigation systems would choose a route that runs further away from the pool. Enter this point to keep you at the pool.

Camping Fontaine Vieille GPS: N44 43.562 W1 04.846
Coq Hardi GPS: N44 42.800 W1 03.683
Camping Le Roumingue GPS: N44 42.354 W1 02.743
Camping Le Braou GPS: N44 41.046 W1 00.260

WP 27: Parc Ornithologique - Le Teich
GPS: N44 38.417 W1 01.180

The nature reserve was created to protect wild birds, but also to allow visitors to see the animals close. On well-marked paths, one can discover on paths more than 15 km long, the 120-acre area, which is characterized by forests, meadows, salt marshes and waterways. There are birds that stay here permanently, but also migratory birds stop here. 260 species were recorded, of which 80 species breed in the park, as well as the white stork.

Camping Ker Helen GPS: N44 38.388 W1 02.572

WP 28: Arcachon - oyster farming
GPS: N44 38.709 W1 08.739

Arachon is the center of oyster farming in France. Many small companies are employed with the breed. The fishing boats are lined up on the ground at low tide, as the tidal rise of the Atlantic is quite high, they can only leave at high tide.

WP 29: Arcachon Plage
GPS: N44 39.797 W1 09.948

With a little luck you can find a parking space on the promenade, otherwise you have to try your luck in the side streets. An RV parking is not available.

The town itself has a wonderful long and wide sandy beach around the center has developed. In the center the pedestrian zone extends down to the sea, and here you can find many restaurants where oysters can be enjoyed.

Of course there is offered the classic oyster from Arcachon, as well as species with gray to greenish flesh called "fines" or "specials".

WP 30: Dune du Pilat - Parking
GPS: N44 35.896 W1 12.021

In front of the dune there is a huge parking lot with shade. From this car park it is 5 minutes to the dune. Right and left of the road there is one restaurant next to the other, in which fish dishes and specialties are offered at relatively moderate prices. Having arrived at the dune, there are ladders to the top. There is a lot of tourists here, because everyone wants to climb the dune. Once at the top, a strong wind often blows, so you should protect your camera equipment.

It is the largest sand dune in Europe and runs from north to south. It is at its highest point up to 117 meters high, 500 meters wide and extends to a length of 2.7 km. On the ocean side, it has a slope of up to 20 °, on the land side up to 40 °. It has a pure sand area of 87 hectares, was put under Conservation in 1978. The sea, the wind, the currents, winds and tides and humans contributed to the development of the dune. Their internal structure suggests that it is formed about 18,000 years ago. Currently due to climate change, the amount of sand transported is lower, the dunes are therefore constantly losing altitude. But the tides and erosion can build further south a new dune.

Camping La Forêt GPS: N44 35.111 W1 12.527
Camping La Dune GPS: N44 34.868 W1 12.749
Camping Pyla GPS: N44 34.684 W1 12.784
Camping Le Petit Nice GPS: N44 34.349 W1 13.247
Vivier GPS: N44 27.533 W1 14.400

WP 31: Biscarosse Plage

GPS: N44 27.144 W1 14.251

Marvellous Beaches around Biscarosse Plage.

WP 32: Biscarosse Plage - Boulevard Des Sables

GPS: N44 26.793 W1 15.335

Biscarosse Plage - Etang de Cazaux - Plage de Viviers - Marqueze - Mimizan - Contis Plage - Saint-Girons - Moliets 204 km

The route now leads inland to several lakes, the Etangs, freshwater lakes, which are mainly used by surfers and sailors who fear the heavy surf of the Atlantic. The small lake attracts because of its calm waters and its temperatures. Idyllic it is situated in the countryside, there are a few hotels and guest houses, as well as campsites. Around the lake, as well as in the ocean, not only here, but also in the nearby Etang de Biscarosse oil is exploited but no fear, those responsible take care that every drop is precious and none is wasted, therefore excellent water quality.

WP 33: Route Des Lacs - Navigation Point

GPS: N44 27.409 W1 12.129

WP 34: Ispe - Navigation Point

GPS: N44 26.354 W1 11.547

Both points are navigation points by which, one drives right along the lake. There are wonderful picnic spots on the lake, which are also suitable for mobile homes, which are also heavily used.

Navarosse GPS: N44 25.917 W1 11.000

Camping Campéole Navarrosse
GPS: N44 25.915 W1 10.131

Village Mayotte Vacances
GPS: N44 26.116 W1 09.298

Camping Les Écureuils
GPS: N44 25.771 W1 10.021

Camping Bimbo
GPS: N44 25.600 W1 09.644

WP 35: Plage de Viviers

GPS: N44 24.015 W1 15.723

Even here on the coast, there are wonderful beach areas, which are well suited for campers.

WP 36: Beach Parentis

GPS: N44 20.738 W1 06.101

On the way to the museum village you will pass the Etang de Biscarrosse, where you should make a stopover. The lakeside rest is equipped with a lawn, toilets and showers. Opposite is the Camping Municipal Pipiou.

Camping Municipal Pipiou
GPS: N44 20.756 W1 06.064

Camping L' Arbre d'Or   GPS: N44 20.773 W1 05.574

WP 37: Sabres - Railway to Marqueze

GPS: N44 09.007 W0 45.768

Directly opposite the railway station there is parking in the shade. The tickets for the train station and the museum village is available at the station. The visit to the village is highly recommended and the approximately 15 minute long train journey in a historic train is an experience not only for kids.

The Open Air Museum displays typical farms in France. After the ride you can make a walking trip on the site, which is about 3 km long and takes you to all the farm houses. A mill was dismantled and rebuilt here. Of interest is the architecture of the houses, and the arrangement of the rooms, usually one enters the building directly to the central kitchen, from where you get to the sleep chambers and storerooms. There is also a bakery shop where you get freshly baked bread and pastries from old recipes.

WP 38: Mimizan-Plage

GPS: N44 12.821 W1 17.566

For campers in Mimizan there is a parking space right next to the dunes at the beach. The fee is relatively high, but there are toilet and beach showers. Unfortunately, it is often overcrowded in the pre season and the asphalt base is not really appealing.

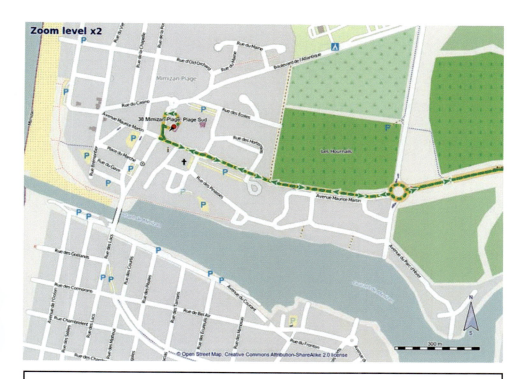

WP 39: Contis-Plage

GPS: N44 05.453 W1 19.308

Very unusual are the buildings in Contis - Plage. Many houses are built directly on the Beach dune and it is surprising that the houses seem to withstand the movement of a dune. Again, there is a paid RV park just a few meters from the sea, with all utilities. Contis - Plage is one of the less-visited beaches as it is missing accommodations in the immediate area, the beach is populated mainly by campers.

Village Lous Seurrots GPS: N44 05.329 W1 18.980

Camping Municipal du Cap de l'Homy
GPS: N44 02.246 W1 20.043

WP 40: Saint-Girons-Plage

GPS: N43 57.141 W1 21.646

WP 41: Etang de Leon - Camping Le Col Vert

GPS: N43 53.220 W1 19.102

Beautiful lake with camping on the lake shore - opposite is an inexpensive restaurant with delicious pizzas.

Camping Le Col Vert GPS: N43 54.197 W1 18.636

Camping Airotel Lou Puntaou
GPS: N43 53.081 W1 18.898

WP 42: Moliets-Plage

GPS: N43 51.116 W1 23.242

Camping Le Saint Martin
GPS: N43 51.176 W1 23.252

Moliets - Vieux-Boucau - Plage Des Casernes - Capbreton - Ondres Plage - Bayonne - Biarritz - St-Jean 98 km

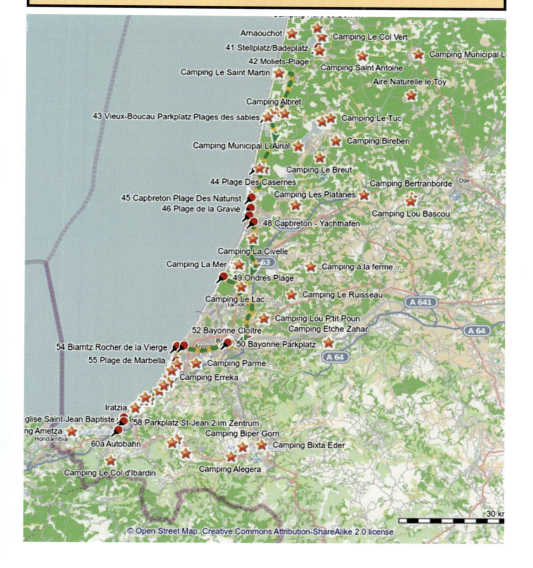

WP 43: Vieux-Boucau - Parking - Plages des Sables

GPS: N43 47.557 W1 24.667

Camping La Côte GPS: N43 48.025 W1 23.512

Camping Le Vieux Port GPS: N43 47.866 W1 24.042

Camping Albret GPS: N43 47.790 W1 23.704

Camping Municipal des Sablères
GPS: N43 47.585 W1 24.364

WP 44: Plage des Casernes

GPS: N43 43.399 W1 25.814

Beautiful beach with large parking lots, and little visited.

Camping Les Oyats GPS: N43 43.493 W1 25.303

Camping Les Chevreuils GPS: N43 43.414 W1 24.775

WP 45: Capbreton-Plage Des Naturiste

GPS: N43 41.056 W1 26.280

Capbreton is one of the larger towns in this section of the coast with a large number of beaches. This is a nude - beach.

WP 46: Capbreton - Plage de la Graviè

GPS: N43 40.206 W1 26.371

WP 47: Capbreton - Plage Sud

GPS: N43 39.644 W1 26.561

WP 48: Capbreton - Yacht Harbour

GPS: N43 39.105 W1 26.065

Capbreton is very popular with sailors, because it has a protected marina. The Atlantic is due to its constant winds a great sailing waters, but unlike the Mediterranean, only for more experienced captains and larger vessels, as the waves are much higher here, stronger winds, and the prevailing currents make sailing somewhat more difficult.

Camping La Civelle GPS: N43 37.825 W1 25.965

Camping Le Lac   GPS: N43 33.961 W1 27.209

WP 49: Ondres Plage

GPS: N43 34.646 W1 29.275

WP 50: Bayonne - Parking

GPS: N43 29.311 W1 28.768

Parking can be found quite difficult in Bayonne, especially for larger camping cars. The best bet might be at Rampart Boulevard Rampart Lachepaillt. The metered parking spaces are usually too small for campers.

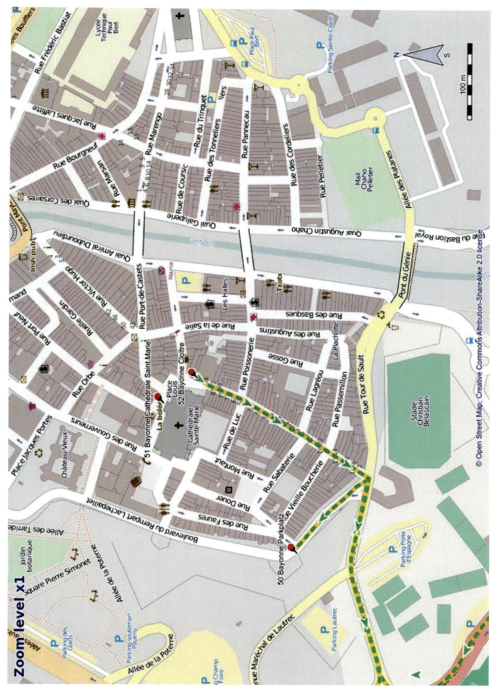

Have you managed to park on Rampart Boulevard Lachepaillt, you are just a few steps away from the center.

WP 51: Bayonne - Cathédrale St. Marie

GPS: N43 29.445 W1 28.613

Worth visiting is the Cathedral of Saint Mary. Small alleys are leading to the center and to the Cathedral of St. Mary from 13th century. Often it was hit in the history by fires, some caused dramatic devastation. Extensive alterations and improvements contributed to today's picture of the Gothic cathedral. Most of the beautiful stained glass windows date from the 16th century. The artfully crafted double doors lead into the sacristy, which dates from the first construction phase, during 13th Century.

WP 52: Bayonne - Cloître - Cloister

GPS: N43 29.422 W1 28.590

The cloister is affiliated with the church dating from the 14th Century and can only be reached from the outside. Late Gothic Flamboyant style catches the eye of the visitor. A long passage is covered by elegant taut arcs, which are composed of intricate rosettes.

Noteworthy are also the beautiful houses on the river Adour and the historic bridges.

WP 53: Biarritz - Grande Plage
GPS: N43 29.098 W1 33.462

What applies to Bayonne with respect to parking, applies to Biarritz much more. The city is hopelessly overcrowded and many times you have to go round in circles until you can finally park the car reasonably well. The Grand Plage is located in the center and is especially popular among young people, because you can reach it by foot from the center. It is a meeting place of the youth.

WP 54: Biarritz - Rocher de la Vierge
GPS: N43 29.031 W1 34.165

Almost a symbol is the Virgin Mary at the Rocher de la Vierge. None other than Mr. Eiffel, the designer of the Eiffel Tower in Paris, created a bridge to the rocks, the main attraction for tourists.

WP 55: Biarritz - Plage de Marbella
GPS: N43 28.060 W1 34.343

Just outside the town is the beach of Marbella, which is well out of reach of Biarritz.

Camping Parme GPS: N43 27.852 W1 31.946

The campsite is located near the airport, from which it is about 2 km to the center. There are buses from the airport to downtown.

WP 56: Biarritz - Plage de la Milady

GPS: N43 27.926 W1 34.309

A few hundred meters from Plage de Marbella there is Milady Beach.
Campsites are available here - an alternative to the campsite at the airport,but from here you need a quarter of an hour to the center of Biarritz.

Camping Biarritz GPS: N43 27.731 W1 34.020

Camping Le Pavillon Royal
GPS: N43 27.275 W1 34.589

Camping Erreka GPS: N43 26.739 W1 34.938

The route now leads along the coast to St-Jean-de-Luz. Numerous bays for a swim - the route is dotted with beaches and, of course, there is the availability of large campsites.

WP 57: Navigation Point

GPS: N43 26.222 W1 35.535

To actually stay on the coast road, one enters the coordinates of POI 57, because otherwise you will be piloted through the hinterland to St-Jean.

Camping Sunêlia Berrua GPS: N43 26.287 W1 34.911

Camping Ur-Onea GPS: N43 26.038 W1 35.444

Camping Le Parc GPS: N43 25.643 W1 35.954

Camping Atlantica GPS: N43 24.941 W1 36.988

Itsas GPS: N43 24.883 W1 37.017
Camping Tamaris Plage GPS: N43 25.076 W1 37.439
Camping Inter Plages GPS: N43 24.900 W1 37.597
Camping Playa GPS: N43 24.858 W1 37.585
Erromardie GPS: N43 24.467 W1 38.267
Iratzia GPS: N43 24.283 W1 38.467

WP 58: St-Jean - Parking

GPS: N43 23.095 W1 39.956

The best idea to park the vehicle is on POI 58 the parking lot at the harbor. The parking fee is not excessive and the vehicle is very safe. However, for larger motorhomes from about 6 feet it is quite narrow. From the parking lot it is a 5 minute walk to the center. Already on the way there, the harbor flatters the eyes, from the bridge you can already see the Musee Grevin, which is housed in the former palace.

WP 59: St-Jean Promenade

GPS: N43 23.351 W1 39.839

Not to be missed is the promenade with the fine sandy beach and the villas that line the promenade. As 1968, the first Baroque and Art Deco villas slated for demolition on the promenade, to make way for apartment blocks, the mayor imposed a building stop, which prevented the destruction of the cityscape.

WP 60: St-Jean - Église Saint-Jean

GPS: N43 23.286 W1 39.765

The Church of St-Jean Baptiste was made famous by a royal marriage. King Louis XIV married the Spanish Infanta Maria Teresa here in 1660, but he did not do so voluntarily. He was in love with the niece of the consultant Mazzarin, a beautiful young woman, but he had to submit to the reason of state, for the marriage to Mary was in the Peace Treaty of the Pyrenees already regulated. An interesting detail, his future wife was his cousin, because HIS mother and HER father were brother and sister and the mother of HIS BRIDE and HIS father were also siblings, not at this time a real impediment to the marriage, if it was the reason of state.
The wedding was held magnificently and with all kinds of ceremonies, the main portal, through which the couple left the church, was bricked right after that and it is still today, only a plaque to commemorate the royal event.

WP 60a: Motorway

GPS: N43 22.373 W1 40.463

This Point of Interest will bring you directly to the motorway A63 direction north.

Printed in Great Britain
by Amazon